TRINITY

VOL.1 BETTER TOGETHER

TRINITY

VOL.1 BETTER TOGETHER

FRANCIS MANAPUL
writer

FRANCIS MANAPUL

EMANUELA LUPACCHINO * RAY McCARTHY * MATT SANTORELLI * CLAY MANN * SETH MANN
artists

FRANCIS MANAPUL

BRAD ANDERSON * HI-FI
colorists

STEVE WANDS
letterer

FRANCIS MANAPUL
collection cover artist

SUPERMAN created by JERRY SIEGEL and JOE SHUSTER.
By special arrangement with the Jerry Siegel family.
BATMAN created by BOB KANE with BILL FINGER.
WONDER WOMAN created by WILLIAM MOULTON MARSTON.

EDDIE BERGANZA Editor - Original Series ✳ **PAUL KAMINSKI** Associate Editor - Original Series ✳ **JEB WOODARD** Group Editor - Collected Editions
PAUL SANTOS Editor - Collected Edition ✳ **STEVE COOK** Design Director - Books ✳ **DAMIAN RYLAND** Publication Design

BOB HARRAS Senior VP - Editor-in-Chief, DC Comics
PAT McCALLUM Executive Editor, DC Comics

DIANE NELSON President ✳ **DAN DiDIO** Publisher ✳ **JIM LEE** Publisher ✳ **GEOFF JOHNS** President & Chief Creative Officer
AMIT DESAI Executive VP - Business & Marketing Strategy, Direct to Consumer & Global Franchise Management
SAM ADES Senior VP & General Manager, Digital Services ✳ **BOBBIE CHASE** VP & Executive Editor, Young Reader & Talent Development
MARK CHIARELLO Senior VP - Art, Design & Collected Editions ✳ **JOHN CUNNINGHAM** Senior VP - Sales & Trade Marketing
ANNE DePIES Senior VP - Business Strategy, Finance & Administration ✳ **DON FALLETTI** VP - Manufacturing Operations
LAWRENCE GANEM VP - Editorial Administration & Talent Relations ✳ **ALISON GILL** Senior VP - Manufacturing & Operations
HANK KANALZ Senior VP - Editorial Strategy & Administration ✳ **JAY KOGAN** VP - Legal Affairs ✳ **JACK MAHAN** VP - Business Affairs
NICK J. NAPOLITANO VP - Manufacturing Administration ✳ **EDDIE SCANNELL** VP - Consumer Marketing
COURTNEY SIMMONS Senior VP - Publicity & Communications ✳ **JIM (SKI) SOKOLOWSKI** VP - Comic Book Specialty Sales & Trade Marketing
NANCY SPEARS VP - Mass, Book, Digital Sales & Trade Marketing ✳ **MICHELE R. WELLS** VP - Content Strategy

TRINITY VOL.1 BETTER TOGETHER

DC Comics, 2900 West Alameda Ave., Burbank, CA 91505
Printed by LSC Communications, Kendallville, IN, USA. 11/10/17. First Printing.
ISBN: 978-1-4012-7466-5

Library of Congress Cataloging-in-Publication Data is available.

PEFC Certified

Printed on paper from
sustainably managed
forests, controlled
sources

PEFC/29-31-337   www.pefc.org

WHEN YOU BECOME A PARENT, A LOT OF PEOPLE ARE GOING TO GIVE YOU THEIR ADVICE.

WHETHER YOU WANT IT OR NOT.

THEN THERE'S THE UNSAID COMPETITION BETWEEN OTHER PARENTS AND THE DEVELOPMENT OF THEIR KIDS.

"MINE IS ONLY FOUR MONTHS OLD AND SHE'S ALREADY CRAWLING!" GOD I HATE THAT.

WELL, MY SON CAN LIFT CARS OVER HIS HEAD. CAN YOU TOP THAT?

LUCKILY, ON TOP OF *MOTHERLY* INTUITION, I WAS ALSO *THE WORLD'S GREATEST REPORTER.* *IT'S MY JOB* TO KNOW THE DIFFERENCE.

--SEVEN BUCKS?! SO I SAID *FORGET IT!* THERE WAS A *GUY* AROUND THE CORNER JUST *GIVING* THEM AWAY! BAGS FULL, MOM! I MEAN HE WAS A LITTLE BIT WEIRD, BUT FREE IS FREE, RIGHT?

I HOPE IT'S OKAY I USED THE MONEY TO GET ICE CREAM.

THAT'S FINE, JUST DON'T TELL YOUR FATHER. SPEAKING OF WHICH, DID YOU DO AS YOUR FATHER SAID?

YES, MOM. I WAS VERY CAREFUL NOBODY FOLLOWED ME HOME. I DIDN'T USE MY POWERS OR NOTHIN'.

I MANAGED TO FIND A SHORTCUT TO TOWN. I WOULD HAVE GOTTEN ALL MY CHORES DONE QUICKER IF I HAD BEEN ABLE TO--

IT'S NOT ABOUT GETTING IT DONE *QUICKLY,* JON. YOU KNOW HOW YOUR FATHER WORRIES.

DING DONG

HUH?

WE *NEVER* GET GUESTS...

I GOT IT!

THIS ISN'T *ME*, DIANA. I DON'T *DO* THIS KIND OF THING.

AND YOU BROUGHT A BOAR?

WILD BOAR.

MY DAD SAID I SHOULD ONLY USE MY POWERS TO KEEP US SAFE. I'M SURE HE'D BE OKAY IF I TOOK A LITTLE PEEK.

JEEZ!

DINNER? *SERIOUSLY?* WE DON'T EVEN KNOW THEM THAT WELL, LOIS.

WHO ARE YOU GOING TO INVITE NEXT, *LEX LUTHOR?*

THAT'S THE WHOLE POINT, CLARK. IF YOU'RE RETURNING TO ACTION...

...I WANT TO KNOW THE PEOPLE WHO WILL HAVE YOUR *BACK.* WE CAN'T REMAIN IN ISOLATION FOREVER. DO IT FOR *JON.*

HERE. TAKE THIS IN, AND SMILE.

THANKS FOR *UH*...COMING, GUYS. I'LL BE HONEST, THIS IS THE LAST THING I EXPECTED.

DIANA MADE ME COME.

YOUR WIFE IS RIGHT, CLARK. THIS NEEDED TO HAPPEN.

I...I'M SORRY I BLASTED YOU, MR. WAYNE. I HOPE MY DAD'S SHIRT FITS OKAY...

THIS IS WHY I LIKE TO WORK ALONE. HAS YOUR FATHER TAUGHT YOU ANYTHING--

DON'T LET HIM INTIMIDATE YOU, JON. BELIEVE ME, BRUCE HAS WORN WORSE THINGS THAN PLAID, AND AS MUCH AS HE TALKS ABOUT WORKING ALONE...

"...I'VE ALWAYS ASSOCIATED *BATMAN* WITH A *ROBIN.*

"I DON'T NECESSARILY AGREE WITH DRAGGING A CHILD INTO THE LINE OF FIRE, BUT I'LL BE HONEST, BRUCE. WHEN DICK'S IDENTITY WAS IN DANGER OF BEING FOUND OUT AFTER HE BROKE HIS ARM, YOU REALLY STEPPED UP TO THE PLATE IN PROTECTING HIM.

"WEARING A *RAINBOW SUIT* TO DRAW ATTENTION AWAY FROM ROBIN...BRILLIANT.

"WHEN DICK TOLD ME THE STORY I JUST ABOUT LOST IT. I DON'T THINK I'VE EVER LAUGHED SO HARD!"

I HAVE **NO RECOLLECTION** OF THIS.

AND IF YOU TRAINED YOUR SON THE WAY I'VE TRAINED MY ROBINS--

A **RAINBOW SUIT**, BRUCE?

HAHAHA HAHAHA!

THIS ISN'T A LAUGHING MATTER, CLARK. UNCHECKED, YOU AND YOUR SON ARE THE **MOST DANGEROUS BEINGS** ON THIS PLANET.

THE SUPERMAN I KNEW LOST BOTH OF HIS PARENTS, AND AS DIFFERENT AS WE WERE...

...WE UNDER-STOOD EACH OTHER.

SKUUUURCH

"WE MAY HAVE GOTTEN OFF TO A SHAKY START, AND SURE, HE MAY HAVE TRIED TO KILL HAL AND ME THE FIRST TIME WE MET...

"...BUT OUR COMMON LOSS HELPED ME UNDERSTAND WHO HE WAS AND WHY HE CHOSE TO PUT ON THE COSTUME.

"HE FOLLOWED THROUGH TO THE VERY END, SACRIFICING HIS LIFE.

"HE WAS A REAL HERO, AND HE WAS ONE OF A KIND."

I WANT YOU TO STOP LOOKING AT ME LIKE THAT, LOIS.

LIKE WHAT?

LIKE A WOUNDED ANIMAL. I'VE DEALT WITH THE LOSS OF *MY* SUPERMAN. I AM NOT HERE TO REKINDLE OLD FEELINGS.

I KNOW, I DIDN'T MEAN TO--

HE IS NOT THE SAME MAN I ONCE LOVED. THOSE FEELINGS NO LONGER RING TRUE. AND TO BE HONEST, MY FEELINGS ARE THE ONLY THING I CAN *TRUST* RIGHT NOW.

I'M *LOST*, LOIS. I CANNOT FIND MY WAY *HOME*.

"THOUGH SHE IS LOSING HER MEMORY OF WHO SHE ONCE WAS, AND GREETED ME AS AN *ENEMY*. TWO FORSAKEN SOULS, LEFT TO WANDER IN THE JUNGLE.

"SHE BLAMES ME FOR WHAT HAS HAPPENED TO HER HUMANITY. THEN SHE BLAMES THE GODS. I REFUSE TO BLAME ANYBODY, INSTEAD I SEEK THE *TRUTH*. WE CONTROL OUR OWN LIVES, AND NO MAN OR GOD CAN WILL IT OTHERWISE.

"I REMINDED HER THAT SHE IS A *WOMAN* AND NOT A BEAST...AND MORE IMPORTANTLY MY *FRIEND*.

"I CAME HERE, LOIS, BECAUSE YOU ARE A STRONG WOMAN, AND I BELIEVE YOU TO BE MY FRIEND. YOU HAVE MANAGED TO START A NEW LIFE IN THIS WORLD WITH YOUR FAMILY, AND IF I WERE TO NEVER FIND MY WAY BACK...

WHAT DO YOU MEAN, DIANA?

I WAS FORCED TO REACH OUT TO AN *OLD FRIEND* FOR HELP.

"...I WANT TO KNOW HOW TO START OVER."

GREAT THINGS START SMALL.

SKLUUUURCH

SKLUUUURCH

SONS GROW UP TO BE FATHERS.

GOOD NIGHT, JON.

FROM STRANGERS TO BROTHERS.

WHEN THEY SLEEP THEY SEEM SO INNOCENT. YOU ALMOST BELIEVE THEY WOULD LISTEN TO WHAT WE SAY.

YOU'LL ALWAYS HAVE A HOME HERE, DIANA.

AND MOST IMPORTANTLY, A FRIEND.

RIVALS TO SISTERS.

I DON'T REGRET RETURNING TO ACTION, BUT I DON'T THINK IT'S THE KIND OF LIFE I WANT FOR MY SON.

PERHAPS THE THREE OF US REUNITING GOES BEYOND JUST DEFEATING THE VILLAINS OF THIS WORLD.

WITH ENOUGH PATIENCE AND UNDERSTANDING, THEIR *FRIENDSHIP* CAN GROW INTO SOMETHING GREATER.

I BELIEVE IN THEM.

DOUBTFUL.

HAH! BELIEVE IT OR NOT, I ACTUALLY AM GLAD YOU BOTH CAME. MAYBE LOIS WAS RIGHT ABOUT--

CLARK!

COME ON, CLARK!

YOU GUYS HEAR THAT?

IT'S COMING FROM INSIDE THE BARN.

TOGETHER THEY CAN BREAK DOWN ANY WALL.

--Uhhh--HE'S STRONG.

WHAT HAVE YOU DRAGGED US INTO, CLARK? WE NEED TO LEAVE. NOW.

NO, BRUCE! NOT UNTIL...

COME ON, DAD...YOU'RE THE STRONGEST MAN I KNOW. PLEASE, WAKE UP!

GENTLE, NOT TOO HARD.

≷Koff! Koff!≷ CLA...CLARK?

I'M HERE...

WHO... THA...THAT EMBLEM...

WONDER WOMAN, TALK SOME SENSE INTO HIM. WE SHOULDN'T BE HERE.

IT'S TOO LATE, BATMAN.

MR. KENT... PLEASE, SLOW DOWN. YOUR HEART--

...AND THAT FACE.

YOU...YOU MUST BE HIS FATHER.

NO... NO... NO!

THERE'S SO MUCH I WANT TO TELL YOU, PA. THERE ARE THINGS I ONLY UNDERSTAND NOW THAT I HAVE A SON OF MY OWN.

I SHARE THE SAME FEARS, THE SAME HOPES AND DREAMS FOR MY OWN SON.

I LOOK AT HIS LITTLE FACE AND SEE YOURS.

I SEE MA'S, TOO.

AND OF COURSE, LOIS. THE FACE OF EVERYONE I'VE EVER LOVED.

EVERYTHING I AM, AND EVERYTHING MY SON WILL BE, IS BECAUSE OF YOU, PA.

I MAY BE SUPERMAN TO THE REST OF THE WORLD, BUT I WANT YOU TO KNOW I AM CLARK KENT.

ADORING FATHER.

LOVING HUSBAND.

PROUD SON.

COCKA-DOODLE-DOOO!

AND IT ALL STARTED ON A QUAINT LITTLE FARM.

Hamilton County.
Now.

OH, JON.

HAVE YOU BEEN THERE ALL NIGHT?

≋YAWN≋ NO, MOM...

WITH ALL THE COMMOTION LAST NIGHT, YOUR FATHER FORGOT TO GIVE YOU THIS.

LISTEN, JON. NOW THAT YOUR FATHER IS BACK AS SUPERMAN, EVERY NOW AND THEN HE'LL MISS WAKING YOU UP IN THE MORNING. BUT NO MATTER WHAT, HE'S ALWAYS FOUND HIS WAY BACK HOME.

AND WHAT HAPPENED LAST NIGHT WASN'T YOUR FAULT. I DON'T WANT YOU TO LIVE IN FEAR OF WHAT'S OUT THERE. THERE'S MORE TO THIS WORLD THAN BAD GUYS TRYING TO TAKE YOU AWAY.

YOUR FATHER AND I WON'T LET ANYTHING HAPPEN TO YOU. NEITHER WILL DIANA AND NEITHER WILL BRUCE. SO I WANT YOU TO STOP WORRYING.

LEAVE THAT TO ME. THAT'S MY JOB, OKAY?

I WILL, MOM.

SNIFF HE'S DEAD...MY DAD IS DEAD BECAUSE OF ME.

HE WAS RIGHT. SNIFF

THOSE STRANGERS WERE HERE TO TAKE ME AWAY. SNIFF

TO TAKE ME BACK TO ANOTHER PLANET.

THIS WAS MY FAULT. NONE OF THIS WOULD HAVE HAPPENED IF--

YOUR FAULT...

SNIFF WHO'S THERE?

HELLO?

WHAT DO I TELL MY FATHER?

THIS IS RIDICULOUS.

I CAN SEE IN BRUCE'S EYES THAT I SHOULD SAY NOTHING.

WE HAVE TO HELP JONATHAN FIND CLARK.

I SEE UNDERSTANDING IN DIANA'S.

I KNOW IT'S A BIT CRAMPED, BUT IMAGINE WHAT PEOPLE WOULD SAY IF THEY SAW THE THREE OF YOU FLYING AROUND DRESSED LIKE THAT.

CURIOSITY IN MY FATHER'S.

IT'S JUST THE WAY I REMEMBER IT.

IT'S BEEN SO LONG SINCE I'VE SEEN SMALLVILLE. IT FEELS FAMILIAR, YET STRANGE. MAYBE IT'S TRUE WHAT THEY SAY ABOUT COMING HOME AGAIN.

I HATE IT WHEN BRUCE IS RIGHT, BUT OUR INTERACTION TODAY COULD CHANGE EVERYTHING. I NEED TO BE CAREFUL WITH WHAT I TELL MY FATHER ABOUT HIS SON.

DEVIL'S MOUTH IS ABOUT TWENTY MINUTES OUT OF TOWN. DESPITE ITS NAME IT REALLY IS QUITE BEAUTIFUL.

I'VE BEEN BRINGING CLARK THERE SINCE HE WAS THREE, TAUGHT HIM HOW TO SWIM THERE. IT WASN'T LONG BEFORE HE WAS DIVING OFF THE ROCKS. HE'D LEAP SO FAR I COULD HAVE SWORN HE COULD FLY.

WE HAVE GOOD MEMORIES THERE. I BET THAT'S WHERE HE'D BE.

THIS PLACE IS BEAUTIFUL, MR. KENT.

THERE'S NO PLACE LIKE IT, SON.

"...LET HIM ENJOY THIS HOMECOMING, BECAUSE IT COULD ALL GO AWAY."

SO ARE YOU GONNA TELL ME ABOUT MY SON OR ARE YOU GONNA KEEP CHEWIN' YOUR TONGUE?

I...WHAT MAKES YOU THINK--

DROP THE ACT, MR. MUSCLES. THE EMBLEM ON YOUR CHEST, THE CARVING ON THE ROCKET SHIP, AND THE RESEMBLANCE...ARE YOU HIS UNCLE OR SOMETHING?

SOMETHING LIKE THAT...

WELL THAT'S A START. YOU HAVE ANY KIDS?

A BOY.

IS HE LIKE YOU? YOU KNOW... DIFFERENT.

YES.

YOU EVER GONNA SPEAK *MORE* THAN FIVE WORDS?

LISTEN, FATHER TO FATHER, LET ME TELL YOU SOMETHING I HOPE YOU'D UNDERSTAND. CAN YOU OUTRUN A TRAIN? LEAP TO ANOTHER TOWN WITH A SINGLE BOUND?

I CAN'T.

EVERYTHING HE IS EXPERIENCING OR FEELING, YOU'VE ALREADY DONE IT. YOU CAN *EXPLAIN* THE WORLD TO HIM IN A WAY I NEVER COULD. YOU CAN *PROTECT* HIM IN A WAY THAT I CAN'T.

FOR YEARS, I'VE BUILT A *WALL* AROUND MY FAMILY TO HELP THEM. IT'S WORKED SO FAR, BUT IT AIN'T GONNA WORK FOREVER.

NOW, YOU AND YOUR FRIENDS HAVE SMASHED THROUGH THAT WALL. AND THAT'S OKAY...I GET IT NOW. IF I WANT TO FIND ANSWERS FOR MY BOY, THE FIRST STEP I'D HAVE TO TAKE IS TO LET OTHERS IN ON THE SECRET.

I...I'M SORRY.

HEY! ARE YOU OKAY?!

...AND YOU CAN'T SWIM.

WHEREVER YOU ARE, HANG ON, CLARK. I'M COMING.

SPLASH

ALL THOSE POWERS...

≥GASP≤ COME ON, UP AND AT 'EM! I GOTTA GET TO MY BOY!

≥KOFF≤ I'M...I'M SO SORRY, MR. KENT.

I CAN'T TELL YOU MUCH ABOUT YOUR SON, BUT THERE ARE THINGS I CAN TELL YOU ABOUT YOU.

YOU'RE ALWAYS UP BEFORE THE SUN RISES TO FEED ALL THE ANIMALS IN THE BARN SO YOUR FAMILY CAN SLEEP IN.

YOU DANCE WITH YOUR WIFE IN THE KITCHEN EVEN THOUGH YOU THINK IT MAKES YOU LOOK SILLY.

YOU ALWAYS WATCH THE SUN SET WITH CLARK BECAUSE IN THAT MOMENT, EVERYTHING ITS LIGHT TOUCHES IS ALL ANYONE COULD EVER WANT.

YOU DON'T HAVE ALL THE ANSWERS, AND YOU DON'T NEED THEM.

EVERYTHING YOU'VE EXPERIENCED, AND EVERYTHING THAT YOU ARE...

...THAT'S ALL HE WILL EVER NEED.

MAN AFTER MAZZ

BETTER TOGETHER Part Three: NOBODY DIES TONIGHT
CLAY MANN, SETH MANN artists * BRAD ANDERSON colorist

NOBODY DIES TONIGHT.

I YELL IT OUT, BUT NO ONE IS LISTENING.

MY FATHER DIED TONIGHT.

KRRRAAAKA-BOOOM

POWER | DARNELL
THE MARK OF ZORRO

MY MOTHER DIED TONIGHT.

...YOU'RE DOING REALLY WELL, BRUCE.

PLEASE CONTINUE.

OKAY...I... I'M RUNNING DOWN THE HALLWAY OF THE MANOR, BUT FOR SOME REASON IT STINKS.

IT SMELLS LIKE POPCORN AND BOILED HOT DOGS.

THERE ARE BATS *EVERYWHERE,* AND THEY'RE COMING AFTER ME.

SUDDENLY I SMELL MY MOTHER'S PERFUME.

I HEAR PEARLS HIT THE FLOOR, AND I FOLLOW THE SOUND.

TIC-TIC-TIC-TIC...

NEXT THING I KNOW, I'M IN A CAVE.

THEN THE LIGHTS GO OUT. I HUDDLE ON THE GROUND.

I...I CA...CAN'T MOVE.

I'M SO SCARED!

EVEN MUNDANE ONES.

LIFE IS ABOUT CHOICES, MASTER BRUCE.

LITTLE ONES. BIG ONES.

IT'S EASY TO THINK THOSE CHOICES LED TO A VERY SPECIFIC OUTCOME--

DON'T, ALFRED.

JUST GIVE ME MY MEDICATION AND LEAVE ME ALONE.

ALFRED... I...

MASTER BRUCE--

NONE OF THIS IS REAL.

IT COULD ALL BE A DREAM.

IF THIS IS TRUE, WHY ARE WE IN CONTROL OF OUR OWN ACTIONS AND OUR OWN THOUGHTS?

FORWARD! I CAN FEEL IT.

THIS REALITY APPEARS TO BE ALTERED BY OUR EMOTIONS. PROVIDING US WITH MOMENTS WE HAVE LONG WANTED... AND RESOLUTIONS WE HAVE ALWAYS NEEDED.

BUT WHY?

AND FOR WHAT PURPOSE?

CLARK HAD AN OPPORTUNITY TO RECONNECT WITH HIS FATHER IN SMALLVILLE. A MUCH NEEDED ENCOUNTER WHICH WOULD HOPEFULLY ALLOW HIM TO TEAR DOWN HIS WALLS AND LET US IN.

BRUCE...POOR BRUCE. HE FAILED TO SEE HIS PARENTS BEFORE THEIR DEATH, BUT I BELIEVE THERE WAS GREATER IMPORTANCE IN FACING *HIMSELF.*

AS FOR ME...

...I AM HERE TO SEEK...

I BREATHE IN THE SALTY OCEAN AIR, AND I AM REMINDED OF FISHING EXCURSIONS WITH KASIA. I FEEL THE GRANULAR SANDS OF THE COLISEUM UNDERNEATH MY FEET, AND REMINISCE OF SPARRING SESSIONS WITH EVRAYLE.

I FEEL AT EASE. I FEEL AT HOME.

THIS FEELS SO...REAL...

‹MY SISTERS OF THEMYSCIRA!›

‹THE PATRONS HAVE BROUGHT UPON OUR SHORES A TEST.›

‹I BELIEVE A PROPER RESPONSE WOULD BE TO DO THE SAME IN RETURN.›

QUEEN HIPPOLYTA. MY MOTHER. SHE VALUES HONOR, STRENGTH AND LOVE.

WE WILL BE WELL.

‹LIFE AND DEATH WILL BE DETERMINED THROUGH YOUR PERFORMANCE IN THE GAMES!›

‹MAY THE PATRONS LOOK DOWN UPON YOU FAVORABLY.›

WHAT'S GOING ON, WONDER WOMAN?

LONG AGO, I PARTICIPATED IN THESE GAMES, EARNING THE RIGHT TO BE EMISSARY TO THE OUTSIDE WORLD.

WE ARE BEING TESTED, SUPERMAN.

I'M GOING TO ASSUME THE STAKES WILL BE HIGH.

ONLY IF YOU VALUE YOUR LIFE, BATMAN.

TODAY IT IS FOR A DIFFERENT PURPOSE.

THAK

WE FIGHT TO STAY.

YES...AND THIS WORLD WAS CREATED FOR US. IT *WANTS* TO LEARN WHO WE ARE.

AND WHAT BETTER WAY THAN TO SEE US AT OUR MOST VULNERABLE MOMENTS.

I AM AFRAID TO SAY THAT YOU ARE RIGHT.

I DON'T REGRET OUR TIME HERE. I [G]OT TO SEE MY [D]AD ONE LAST TIME...

BUT IT'S ALL A *LIE*.

WE CAN'T BELIEVE ANYTHING WE'VE SEEN.

WHAT ABOUT WHAT WE HAVE *FELT*?

THAT MAY BE THE ONLY TRUTH WE *NEEDED.*

WE'LL HOLD THEM BACK--

YAAAH!

I KNOW WHAT BRUCE IS GOING TO SAY.

THE POSSIBILITY OF ETERNAL DAMNATION GIVES EVERYONE A PAUSE FOR THOUGHT.

DIANA!

IT'S OKAY. WE'RE FREE.

I KNOW YOUR MOTHER OFFERED YOU THE CHANCE TO STAY, BUT YOU CHOSE TO LEAVE WITH US.

I JUST WANTED TO SAY--

BUT I CAN SEE IT IN HIS HEART. HE WILL MEAN IT.

EVEN IF IT'S IN ANOTHER WORLD.

MY NAME IS PAMELA ISLEY, BUT I PREFER TO BE CALLED **POISON IVY.**

I AM A CHOSEN PROTECTOR FOR SOMETHING CALLED THE GREEN. IT'S AN ELEMENTAL FORCE WHICH CONNECTS ALL PLANT LIFE...

...AND RECENTLY IT'S GIVEN ME THE GIFT TO CONSCIOUSLY ENTER MY OWN DREAMS.

UP UNTIL NOW, I WAS THE ONLY NON-PLANT LIFE-FORM IN THIS PLACE...

THIS WAR-BORN CHILD LOOKED AT ME WITH SURPRISING INNOCENCE.

I DIDN'T KNOW WHERE SHE--OR IS IT A HE--CAME FROM.

I TAUGHT HER HOW TO CREATE LIFE.

HOW TO LOVE.

...THEN EVERYTHING CHANGED.

ALL I KNEW IS THAT *SHE* NEEDED ME.

BUT AFTER RECENT EVENTS...I NEEDED *HER* MORE.

THEN I WAS TAKEN AWAY.

AWAKENED FROM MY PERFECT WORLD.

"...AND *BOREDOM*.

"HERE IN THE BLACK MERCY'S WORLD OF FANTASY AND WISH FULFILLMENT, I'VE KILLED YOU A MILLION TIMES OVER, SUPERMAN.

"BUT I HAD THIS FEELING, SCRATCHING ME FROM THE INSIDE... WANTING TO GET OUT.

"SOMETHING WAS MISSING.

"I'D GOTTEN WHAT I WANTED...

"...BUT NOT WHAT I *NEEDED*.

"THAT'S WHEN MY WHITE MERCY WAS BORN!

"I CAN'T EXPLAIN HOW, BUT THIS PLACE GIFTED ME AN HEIR...

"...A CHILD CAPABLE OF CHANNELING NOT ONLY THE DREAMS OF THIS WORLD, BUT THE *NIGHTMARES* AS WELL."

"I IMPARTED MY KNOWLEDGE OF TAKING LIVES.

"AND HOW TO CONQUER!

"WHAT I FELT WAS INDESCRIBABLE! I FELT TRUE HAPPINESS.

"MY WORLD WAS PERFECT."

"THEN ONE DAY, OUR WORLD WAS BREACHED BY AN OUTSIDER.

"THIS *POISON IVY'S* APPEARANCE REVEALED THE TRUE NATURE OF OUR REALITY--MY CHILD AND I WERE PRISONERS IN A DREAM.

"SO WE GAINED HER TRUST, AND EVEN HER LOVE. WHEN SHE GOT EVERYTHING SHE NEEDED, SHE LET HER GUARD DOWN AND REVEALED HER SECRETS.

"THIS ENTIRE WORLD IS A CREATION OF THE BLACK MERCY PLANT, AND HER CONNECTION TO SOMETHING CALLED THE *GREEN* ALLOWED HER TO ACCESS IT.

"SHE WAS GOING TO BE OUR SALVATION."

FIRST I NEEDED TO SEND HER BACK TO YOUR WORLD.

YOU GAVE POISON IVY WHAT SHE NEEDED...AS YOU HAVE GIVEN US.

WE'RE YOUR MEANS OF ESCAPE...

NOT IF WE HAVE ANYTHING TO SAY ABOUT IT!

IT'S TOO LATE, SUPERMAN.

EACH OF YOU HAVE ALREADY LET *ME* INTO YOUR HEARTS.

I WAS THE MYSTERIOUS VOICE THAT BROKE DOWN YOUR WALLS.

I WAS THE DOCTOR THAT LISTENED TO YOUR DEEPEST FEARS.

AND FOR A BRIEF MOMENT. I WAS EVEN YOUR FAMILY.

YOUR BODIES ARE EMPTY VESSELS IN THE OUTSIDE WORLD, SUPERMAN.

THE POWERS OF THE SUN BURSTING THROUGH YOUR BODY WILL ENSURE MY CHILD'S DOMINANCE OVER YOUR WORLD.

"MY FATHER TOLD ME THEY'RE EARTH'S GREATEST HEROES...YET I WAS ABLE TO DEFEAT THEM WITHOUT STRIKING A *SINGLE BLOW.*

"THEIR ATTACHMENTS TO THOSE THEY LOVE DICTATE THEIR ACTIONS.

"THEY EVEN PUT ON A BRAVE FACE, THOUGH THEIR BIGGEST FEAR LIES *WITHIN.*

"THEY HARBOR THE BLAME FOR THINGS THEY DON'T HAVE CONTROL OVER...

"...AND STRUGGLE TO MAKE SENSE OF THE THINGS THEY *DO.*

"DESPITE ALL OF THEIR HUMAN FAILINGS..."

"...WE ENVY THEM, AS THEY EXIST IN THE REAL WORLD.

"ALTHOUGH RIGHT NOW, WE ARE IN MY FATHER'S DREAM.

"IT GIVES THE DREAMERS WHAT THEY WANT.

"OUT OF NECESSITY, THE BLACK MERCY CREATED *ME*...

"USING SUPERMAN'S BODY AS A VESSEL, I HELPED MY FATHER, *MONGUL,* ESCAPE INTO THE REAL WORLD.

LISTEN TO ME, CHILD.

YOUR FATHER HAS ABANDONED YOU. IF YOU TELL US WHAT HE IS PLANNING, WE CAN HELP YOU--*SUPERMAN?!*

THDD

ENOUGH WITH THESE GAMES! YOU'VE PLAYED WITH OUR EMOTIONS, AND NOW YOU'VE UNLEASHED A MONSTER INTO THE REAL WORLD!

TELL US HOW TO GET OUT OF HERE. *NOW!*

YOUR FRIEND IS DYING.

THIS WORLD WILL CONSUME HIS MIND AS MY FATHER TAKES OVER HIS BODY.

I CAN HELP.

I BROUGHT EACH OF YOU INTO YOUR OWN PASTS IN ORDER TO BREAK DOWN YOUR EMOTIONAL BARRIERS. IT WAS THE ONLY WAY WE COULD GET THROUGH TO YOU.

MY FATHER WANTED *OUT* OF THIS PLACE, AND I NEEDED TO BE REUNITED WITH MY MOTHER. POSSESSING YOU THREE WAS THE ONLY WAY WE COULD MAKE THAT HAPPEN.

BUT SOMETHING *UNEXPECTED* HAPPENED INSTEAD.

"I EXPERIENCED THE *JOY* IN SUPERMAN'S HEART FROM REUNITING WITH HIS FATHER.

"I KNEW THE *LOYALTY* WONDER WOMAN DISPLAYED BY CHOOSING HER FRIENDS OVER HER OWN PERSONAL PARADISE.

"AND YOU, BATMAN. I FELT THE *WEIGHT* OF YOUR REGRET, BUT ALSO THE STRENGTH THAT YOU DREW FROM THAT TRAUMA.

"I FELT ALL OF IT."

THE ENTIRE SPECTRUM OF EMOTIONS WHICH MY FATHER CONSIDERED A WEAKNESS, I NOW REALIZE MADE YOU ALL STRONGER.

I EXPERIENCED YOUR HEARTBREAK, YOUR FAILURES AND TRIUMPHS, AND WHAT YOU DO IN ITS AFTERMATH. I ENVY YOUR ABILITY TO LOVE OUTSIDE OF YOURSELF AND ACT SELFLESSLY.

MY GOAL WAS TO STUDY THE THREE OF YOU, BUT IN DOING SO YOU HELPED ME UNDERSTAND WHAT IT'S LIKE TO BE HUMAN. TO BE REAL.

THE CHILD IS BEING SINCERE, BATMAN.

HRM...IF YOU UNDERSTOOD WHAT IT'S LIKE TO BE US, THEN WHY DID YOU HELP MONGUL?

BECAUSE WE CAN'T DEFEAT HIM IN HERE, BATMAN.

UNLIKE MY FATHER, I WILL NOT TAKE YOUR BODY BY FORCE. I CAN FEEL WONDER WOMAN'S TRUST GROWING, AND HER PART TO PLAY IS IN HERE.

YOURS IS OUT THERE. WILL YOU LET ME IN, BATMAN?

"TOGETHER, WE CAN DEFEAT MONGUL."

DAD! I'M SO SORRY--

NICE SHOT, KID! SMALL-TOWN FOLKS, BIG-TOWN SECRETS, HUH?

AND REMEMBER, THAT'S NOT YOUR FATHER. HIS BODY IS STILL POSSESSED BY THE MONSTER FROM THE DREAM WORLD.

AND HE'S BAD NEWS.

CLARK! IT'S US! PLEASE WAKE UP!

I DON'T THINK DAD'S LISTENING, MOM.

I UNDER-
STAND THEM
NOW.

I FEEL
IT, MOTHER.
LOVE.

THIS BODY
HAS OTHERS WHO
CARE FOR HIM, AS WELL.
I CAN'T DEPRIVE HIM OF
THE SAME LOVE I FEEL
FOR YOU RIGHT NOW.

MY DEAR
DAUGHTER,
DON'T...

YOU WON'T
SUFFER ANY
HEARTACHE,
MOTHER.

THROUGH
MY CONNECTION
TO THE GREEN,
I WILL MAKE YOU
FORGET.

NO--

REMEMBER
WHAT YOU
TAUGHT ME?

MOTHER
EARTH
ALWAYS
FINDS A WAY
TO SURVIVE.

BATMAN
HAS AWOKEN,
THEY ARE BOTH
SAFE.

MY ABILITY
TO SEE THE
TRUTH...

BATMAN ★ WONDER WOMAN ★ SUPERMAN

TRINITY

VARIANT COVER GALLERY

TRINITY #1 Variant Cover by JASON FABOK and BRAD ANDERSON